Achieve Peace through Ancient Wisdom and Modern Science

Body-Centered, Somatic Psychotherapy

By

Barry Gray

Achieve Peace through Ancient Wisdom and Modern Science

ISBN: 9781977036476

Warning and Disclaimer

Every effort has been made to make this book as accurate as possible. However, no warranty or fitness is implied. The information provided is on an "as-is" basis. The author and the publisher shall have no liability or responsibility to any person or entity with respect to any loss or damages that arise from the information in this book.

Hakomi™ is the trademarked property of Hakomi Institute. Use of a trademark in this book should not be regarded as affecting the validity of any trademark or service mark. The Publisher is not affiliated, associated, authorized, endorsed by, or in any way officially connected with Hakomi Institute, or any of its subsidiaries or its affiliates. The use of trademarked names is strictly for editorial and descriptive purposes, and no commercial claim to their use, or suggestion of sponsorship or endorsement, is made by the Publisher. Reference to any specific commercial product, process, or service by trade name, trademark, manufacturer, or otherwise [including links to other sites] does not necessarily constitute or imply its endorsement, recommendation, or favoring by the Publisher.

Publisher Contact

Skinny Bottle Publishing

books@skinnybottle.com

How to Combine Eastern and Western Concepts to Achieve Mindfulness **1**

Chapter 1 .... *3*

The Origins of Hakomi. **3**

Chapter 2 .... *9*

The Basic Principles to be Aware of. **9**

Chapter 3 .... *17*

How it Could Benefit Your Life. **17**

Chapter 4 .... *25*

The Branches of Hakomi. **25**

Chapter 5 .... *31*

How it Works. **31**

Chapter 6 .... *39*

Getting Started **39**

Chapter 7 .... *45*

Breaking it Down Into Small Steps. **45**

Chapter 8 .... *55*

The Flow. **55**

Chapter 9 .... *61*

Understanding the Method. **61**

Conclusion. **67**

How to Combine Eastern and Western Concepts to Achieve Mindfulness

The world today appears to just be chaotic no matter the direction in which you turn. This in itself is rather depressing and it's no surprise to discover that all of this chaos leads to an increase in health conditions both physical and mental.

I feel that this is an issue that we are actually starting to come to terms with, and it's about time too. We have to realise that we just cannot keep carrying on in the way that we are or else we will all crumble at different times. If you think about the way in which the Internet fires information all over the world in an instant with it getting busier and busier, then it is easy to start to think about your mind as doing the same thing.

So, what do we do?

For me, the only way to correctly tackle this issue of the chaos in our mind is to do so head-on. There is just no other way to deal with it that can ultimately be as effective. However, I do understand that this can be a scary and intimidating approach to take, which is why we have to look at somehow softening the blow that our psyche can take. After all, suddenly deciding that you will no longer allow the chaos and noise to reign supreme in your mind is, in itself, a stressful event.

I too have found myself in this very situation, but then as I searched online for answers it also became clear that so many approaches focused on the mental aspect alone. You may even be familiar with the idea of mindfulness, or perhaps you have even tried it before as this is regarded as being one of the more popular ways to approach this issue.

But, I have a slight problem with it.

Yes, mindfulness does work; it has been scientifically proven over and over again, but for me there is a need to go further. You see, there is a strong link between the mind and how it then affects the body physically. They both go hand in hand. That means you have to be prepared to tackle things in both realms if you are going to stand the best possible chance of overcoming the chaos, noise and stress in your mind.

Now, I understand that some people may very well think that mindfulness can achieve that, and for some people it does. However, I'm going to discuss a different approach. An approach that does incorporate the basic concepts of mindfulness, but one that goes further.

To do that, I am going to move you around the world and look at a method that combines both Western and Eastern philosophies. A method that tackles this very subject from so many different angles that it is easy to see how it can ultimately prove to be rather effective.

That method is known as Hakomi, and by the end of this book it may very well be the thing that completely alters your perception on life.

Chapter 1

The Origins of Hakomi

As this is going to be a new term for you to try to comprehend, it makes sense for me to kick things off by looking at the origins. After all, you will want to know where it comes from before you go ahead and place your faith in its approaches, don't you? The good news is that it is far easier to understand than you would expect.

The origins of the Hakomi method goes back to the 1970's and a guy called Ron Kurtz. Ron actually had a background in science, mathematics and computing, but as a result it led to him becoming interested in the systems theory. Eventually, he moved to San Francisco where he had graduate training in experimental psychology, which would then ultimately lead to the development of his Hakomi form of therapy.

The Incorporation of Systems.

Due to his analytical mind and scientific background, Ron was constantly fascinated with the way in which different systems could integrate with one another. Through reading, he became intrigued with various areas of the mind and how we can heal both it and the body via a series of different methods. For him, each method and approach was akin to an individual system, and he would begin to study how aspects of each system could be integrated to produce a more thorough and complete approach.

With these systems, his primary attention was psychological change as well as how it can heal the body. Furthermore, his studies on mindfulness and its therapeutic benefits also began to creep into his new methodology. Adding in a concept of non-violence and also the evolution of our conscious mind, the Hakomi Method began to evolve into its very own combination of approaches that utilised different ideas from around the world.

As we go through the book, you will begin to develop a better understanding of the different systems combined with the methodology that Ron had absolute faith in when putting this method together. The Hakomi Method may very well incorporate different aspects from various philosophies, but as you will soon see, it has the same basic things in each step that you will then have to take when employing the method.

However, enough of the actual origins as you are reading this to understand how you can incorporate it into your life. So, I will just address one final point in this chapter that is probably bugging you, and that is where the word itself even originates.

The Meaning of the Word 'Hakomi'.

I would like to just take a moment to discuss the meaning of the word 'Hakomi' and where it comes from. There is often a misunderstanding in that people are of the opinion it is going to be Eastern in origin as it sounds like it. However, that's not the case as the word itself comes from the Hopi Indian language rather than anywhere near China or Japan.

For most individuals, the word refers more to a saying rather than just one single word. To those that are involved in the Hakomi style of therapy, it refers to an ancient way of asking yourself 'Who are you?' which, as you can see, is going to form an integral part of your ability to make progress with your therapy.

Is it an Effective Form of Psychotherapy?

I feel the need to address this question in the first chapter because most people will be reading this book in the hope of finding some answers to issues that they are perhaps having in their life.

Ultimately, the extent to which any form of psychotherapy is effective does depend on you as the individual and how much effort you put into it. There are times where it is just not going to work for you, but that is not to say that the method itself is faulty, and nor are you. Instead, it just means that the answers you are seeking or the problems that you need resolved are just not compatible with this method. However, as you will see throughout the book, the very fact that the Hakomi Method looks at both the body and the mind, along with incorporating a number of different philosophies and other psychotherapy approaches does mean that it is far more encompassing than other methods or approaches out there. Hopefully, by the time you reach the end of this book you will feel that you are in a much better position to conclude as to whether or not this method is something that you can work with or not.

In Which Settings is it Applied?

I also believe that it makes a lot of sense to look at where this form of psychotherapy can be applied. After all, if you can link this therapy with your own situation, then it is already going to help you to begin to believe that it may very well be the way forward.

The Hakomi Method has been used in a variety of settings from group therapy to individual therapy as well as with couples. Due to its approach, along with its flexibility, it can be useful as either a short-term or long-term solution, but this is going to vary according to the problems that need to be addressed.

But this is the part that may surprise you somewhat, the Hakomi Method can be applied in situations that are outwith the usual auspices of therapy. Instead, individuals have been able to use its teachings in areas such as resolving conflicts, relationship help, mediation situations, even dance or poetry.

In addition, the way in which it helps to improve your thought processes also means that it has helped athletes, business people, life coaching, the list goes on. Basically, anything that we do where our thoughts are able to influence us, either in a positive or negative way, can be helped by this method.

Of course, we cannot forget that the Hakomi Method can be used alongside other forms of therapy especially with the way in which it looks more at the present than the past. For some individuals, this can ultimately lead to a substantial breakthrough that allows them to make the kind of progress that they had been hoping for all along.

So, I feel that this is enough background information as you have hardly decided to purchase this book just to learn the history. Instead, you want to get into the real meat of what it is going to be able to offer you, and how it will help you to make progress in both your thoughts and emotions. With that in mind, it's best that we make a start.

Chapter 2

The Basic Principles to be Aware of

As I mentioned in the previous chapter, Hakomi combines different ideas from a range of philosophies as well as scientific approaches. However, to help you better understand how it can potentially make a difference to your life and way of thinking, I need to cover what are seen by practitioners as being the basic principles of the method.

The one thing that I would like to stress is that it is not as complicated as you perhaps think. Let's face it, there would be no point in something connected to mindfulness and making you feel less stressed being too complex that it then increases your stress levels. However, by just starting things off by looking at these principles, it will then allow you to make a better decision as to whether or not this is something that you would like to perhaps use in your own life.

I must stress that these principles may very well lie at the heart of the method, but they are not set in stone or there to trip you up. They are more of a guidance rather than a set of rules, but it makes sense that if you are able to navigate your way through this therapy while sticking as close to the principles as possible that you will ultimately have a better chance of getting the kind of end results you were hoping for.

So, what is at the core of the method?

Looking at Your Own Self.

Therapy often comes with a problem, and that problem is focused almost entirely on people starting things off on the wrong foot. They have this misconception that it is to do with the mind and that you are seeking to become the kind of person that your mind is telling you to be.

However, that is wrong.

Within the Hakomi method, the approach is to primarily spend some time trying to get to the absolute heart of your own self and largely ignoring what the intellect is trying to tell you. Therapy is not about trying to get to a set end goal that has been pre-determined. Instead, this method sees it as being more of a voyage of discovery where you learn more and more as you go along.

There is a strong requirement for you to be able to connect with what are regarded as being the deepest emotional aspects of your being throughout the process. Of course, you might be automatically sitting there trying to think about what they are before you even begin, so you are in essence falling back into the same old trap as before.

To the founders of this method, the entire basis of psychotherapy should be one where you explore new avenues within your own self with you being led down paths that you never even knew existed. Through this form of therapy, you will be able to identify new aspects of your personality and an awareness of what you enjoy, as well as what you hate, and once you emerge into the other side, you will be able to breathe more easily and look at your future as being one that has a greater sense of hope.

But then, it is all fair and well stating that these are the ideas, and that you need to turn your view inwards to then see the external world in a better light, but you clearly still need to know how to achieve this. That is the direction we will head

Body-Centered Psychotherapy.

Just before I go into the different key principles, I want to quickly mention something else that lies at the core of this entire method, and that is the concept of body-centered psychotherapy.

This in itself is nothing new, but the way in which the Hakomi Method uses these different ideas from various philosophies from around the world is certainly new.

Previously, the world of psychotherapy focused on issues connected to the past with the works of Freud being regarded as key. However, that approach has changed over the last few decades to the point where there is a greater understanding of needing to look at methods of releasing emotion and dealing with the present rather than effectively dwelling on the past. One important point is that it is difficult to deal with issues from your past if your current emotions or situations are themselves out of control.

Introducing the Concept of Principles.

Hakomi therapy has a number of key principles that lie at the core of the entire approach. As I have already mentioned, it will then provide you with the foundations upon which you can build your therapy and improve your life. At this moment, there are five basic principles that you need to be aware of, and I will look at each one independently.

Having a better understanding of each one is key to achieving whatever it is that you wish to get from this therapy. However, as was mentioned earlier, you should not venture into this with pre-conceived ideas simply because these principles will allow you to explore and discover what is actually important for you.

Mindfulness.

The first principle is mindfulness, and I am starting off with this one as it is perhaps the point that most people are going to understand, at least on a basic level. Within the Hakomi method, there is a point of view that mindfulness is about slightly more than just trying to become aware of turning our attention inwards regarding an experience rather than outwards.

Mindfulness itself stems from different aspects of Buddhism, so we immediately see the Eastern philosophies making an appearance in the method. It is regarded as being a certain state of consciousness, but it is relaxed, meditative, non-hypnotic, and a method by which you can explore your own thoughts in a peaceful state.

Of course, mindfulness is something that more people are now familiar with as it has been a bit of a buzz term for a number of years. The positive impact of it is also fully understood along with its known health benefits, so it is understandable how it forms an integral part of this entire method.

But then, why should it play such a key role at all? Well, that is due to the way in which it allows you to change your understanding of so many aspects of your core personality and central thought processes that have often clouded your ability to make a clear call as to what is best for your own self. You must also understand that our first thoughts are generally those that are merely habit, and the same can be said for the actions that we undertake. We do them almost as if we are robots, and yet our thoughts and actions may not be accurately representing our true feelings and opinions. That is where mindfulness helps.

By adopting this method, it allows you to move beyond those robotic thoughts and delve deeper into our inner self; the self that is home to what is actually important to us. This is more important than you realize simply because we tend to restrict ourselves by what are nothing more than historical representations of our life. Moments that have already happened to us feel safe, to a certain extent, whereas mindfulness seeks to push us beyond those self-induced limitations that are holding us back like an invisible straight-jacket.

So, in this instance, mindfulness is more about moving beyond those limits and finding out what lies beneath. It's not easy, but there can be little doubting the potential rewards that can come from being able to achieve mindfulness in this manner.

Mind-Body Holism.

The mind-body holism approach is one of the foundations of the entire Hakomi Method. Without it, we would struggle to make sense of what the therapy is trying to teach us, and there is no way that the method would have ever been able to establish itself without this part of its approach. Some also prefer to refer to it as a mind and body integration if the idea of holism sounds too alien to you.

For those involved in Hakomi, the body is regarded as being an accurate and constant reflection of the beliefs that we hold deep inside our mind and soul. It also reflects our ability to organise our life along with the way in which we tend to act in the world.

This does sound rather heavy to try to discuss, but as it does lie at the absolute root of Hakomi, then I need to provide you with a simple explanation as to how it all pulls together. Only then will you see that the connection that exists between both body and mind

There is undoubtedly a connection between our body and mind. Our body has a tendency to reflect what we are thinking and saying, which is why body language is regarded as being so important to learn and understand. If your mind is telling you that you are depressed, then your body has a tendency to be hunched over. The same applies if you are stressed as it creates tension in the mind, so it makes sense that there would then be tension in your body.

Organicity.

The last principle is organicity, and this is clearly something that most people are not going to understand at the outset. From a Hakomi therapy perspective, organicity refers to a point whereby each of the individual parts are able to communicate with each other as a whole. This happens best when there is no additional pressure or time constraints placed upon it. Instead it occurs naturally and in its own time with the outcome being far more beneficial.

This act of effective self-governance and regulation means that you have been able to move beyond those habitual moments that have so far ruled your actions. Furthermore, when these individual aspects are indeed communicating together, then there is a new sense of inner wisdom that can then drive you forward onto a path that will prove to be more beneficial for your self.

Within Hakomi, there is a sense that this development has to occur organically and without time constraints being placed upon the individual. The practitioner also has to have faith in the individual and that they will indeed eventually find this path all on their own as it is always a journey that is being undertaken. For the practitioner, there should never be a time where they are pushing the agenda or their own opinions on others. Instead, they are merely there to offer advice as the client seeks to venture forth all on their own.

Nonviolence.

At first, it may appear to be rather bizarre that the idea of nonviolence is actually included as a principle as surely this stands without any need for it to be mentioned all on its own? Well, that would only be true if you have jumped to a conclusion as to what this entails as the Hakomi Method has a tendency to not look at things through normal eyes.

In this instance, the concept of nonviolence is different in that it primarily refers to the way in which you explore your own beliefs as part of this process. In order to do so, the Hakomi Method stresses that it should be done in a safe manner and you are required to acknowledge those beliefs that are now viewed as being resistant to your future aims.

The problem with other approaches is that these areas of resistance are often tackled in a forceful manner, but that is not the approach that is used here. Rather than seeing them in this way, the Hakomi Method prefers to view them as opportunities for you to learn from the wisdom that these organic blocks, or thought processes, have contained within them. You must remember that they have been put there for a reason, and rather than confronting them in an aggressive manner, you should seek to understand them and effectively thank them for their presence and the role that they played in your life.

Unity.

The final principle to look at is referred to as 'unity' and the term is pretty self-explanatory as to the direction in which we are now heading. Within the method, there is a firm understanding that we are a combination of different components which not only create us as humans, but are also part of other systems that are even greater in size than our own being.

The system itself is rather particular in nature. There is an understanding that the individual systems that ultimately create our own self form an integral part of the world in general. For example, if you merely look at the systems in question, then you will see that the Hakomi Method refers to things such as the family system, culture, metabolic, spiritual, intrapsychic and interpersonal which can all play a key role in our development.

Bringing the Chapter to an End.

By studying the five principles of the Hakomi Method, the idea is that you can see the absolute roots of the methodology and it will then prove to be easier to incorporate them into your life. Of course, one still requires some guidance at the outset to then be able to take full advantage, but that is what we are now going to turn our attention to.

Overall, I would strongly recommend that you read over the basic concepts of the different principles and just make sure that you follow what each point is really telling you. Remember, there is no correct or incorrect answer as this is your own personal journey, but see this as your starting point from where you can indeed go on to do amazing and wonderful things.

Chapter 3

How it Could Benefit Your Life

Prior to actually delving further into the different aspects of this particular approach, I feel a strong need to discuss how it could potentially benefit your life. Let's face it, you are hardly going to want to dedicate time and effort to something if you have no idea what your end goal is supposed to be.

To be honest, this is quite an easy point to discuss, and the reason for that is the way in which Hakomi can benefit you in any way that you see fit. Now, I do accept that it sounds as if this is putting itself across as being a single solution for all of our ills, but it is due to those basic principles discussed earlier that means this is an accurate statement. The only other thing to mention at this point is simply that it will only be able to benefit your life if you work at it as this does not just come to you with minimal effort.

The Problem with Our Life.

In order for something to benefit us, we need to be aware of the problems that it would then be helping or we may never be aware that there is an issue. In this instance, we are talking about our life in general, although for some there may be some very specific points that are giving them cause for concern.

In the modern world, there is a tendency for us to rush into things without giving much thought to any of our actions. It is only with hindsight that we end up regretting something that we have said or some action that we were responsible for, but by then the moment has long gone.

In addition, stress levels and the speed at which we allow ourselves to think have both increased along with the demands that we allow modern-day life to place upon us. We do not give ourselves the time to think or to weigh up options before ultimately deciding on the best one to take. We allow our body and mind to become swamped with stress and pressure to such an extent that it causes us various illnesses that could end up staying with us the rest of our life.

But here is the one major mistake that people make. They believe that all of this is caused by something over which they have no control. They believe decisions are made for them, and that they need to think or act in a certain way that has been governed by those surrounding them or society in general.

They are not being who they actually want to be. In fact, the very idea of being able to do this is so alien that it too induces a certain degree of stress or depression when we then believe we are unable to run with our goals.

Well, perhaps that is all about to change thanks to employing the Hakomi Method and the various principles that form the core of its existence.

The Long-Term Goal.

Within the Hakomi Method, there is the belief that you should be working on long-term goals if you are to benefit from this approach. To do this, there is the need to focus on aspects of organising the experience as you are having it at this moment, hence the use of mindfulness throughout the approach, and a need to think more carefully about how we actually do what we do.

I know that, at first, this in itself could sound confusing, but I will explain it as we work through this book together.

However, at this juncture, I need to say that by looking at the present and coming to terms with the way in which we do things, the Hakomi Method will seek to help you deal with those core beliefs that we all carry that could be limiting us. Too often, we gloss over those beliefs that lie at the heart of who we are, and even though they may be rooted in the past, it is best for us to come to terms with how it is affecting us at this exact moment in time.

To do this, you need to truly get in touch with your own self. You need to become aware of your own thoughts and feelings at this point and to largely ignore all of the noise that tends to influence our way of thinking. Our own subconscious mind is good at doing this, but by blocking out that interference it does allow us to get to grips with the true essence of what is happening in our lives and mind.

Breaking Through Barriers of Our Mind.

Even though external problems can stop us in our tracks, it is true to say that we have a tendency to be our own worst enemy. Our mind has an amazing ability to trip us up or hold us prisoner purely thanks to the power of our thoughts, and that in itself can be terrifying.

Psychotherapy, in all of its forms, looks to break through those barriers, so it's hardly surprising to discover that the Hakomi Method also makes an attempt.

Our incorrect core beliefs can be looked upon as being a road. At first, that incorrect belief is not as strong as it is now as it starts off as a simple path through a grass field. If you do not then repeat that belief or make those choices, then the path becomes overgrown again and it doesn't have an impact on you.

However, repeat it over and over again and that innocent belief will then work its way into becoming a core belief as it develops from that trodden down path in grass to an 8 lane super-highway with all of the fancy trimmings.

But why do we allow that to happen?

There are a number of reasons as to why this is the case, but to be honest that's not the important part in all of this. Instead, I need us to focus on how we start to create that new path which will ultimately lead to the development of a pathway that is far more beneficial to our future.

With the Hakomi Method, there is the belief that the only way in which this change is able to occur is to do so with effectively kid gloves. The entire process is regarded as being quite delicate, so care has to be taken for it to be a success, Nobody said that this was going to be easy, but I don't want you to worry or fear that you need to have some degree in psychology for it to work as that's not the case.

I will discuss the important steps that you need to take in a later chapter, but just to give you some insight as to the direction in which I'm heading, I will give you a few key points that I just want to float around inside of your mind until you get further into the book.

- By organising the experience, you can bring core beliefs into your conscious mind.
- By doing so, you can then work on establishing healthier beliefs.
- This only occurs under certain conditions that lie at the heart of the Hakomi Method.
- You must feel safe.
- You must incorporate mindfulness into your life.
- You must be aware of the mind-body interaction.
- The ability to pay attention to living in the present.
- Don't rush things or stress as this is an organic process that takes time.

A List of Benefits of Using the Hakomi Method.

The Hakomi Method has been linked to helping individuals break through a number of difficult points in their life. It has also been shown to have been the driving force behind different people being able to make substantial progress when they were previously left feeling as if they were swimming against the tide.

What I would like to do is to just list a number of benefits that are associated with this method. I am not saying that you are going to be guaranteed to get these benefits as that is impossible to do, but the main reason why I want to list them is simply to give you hope. Let's fact it, if other individuals who are in a similar vein of thought as you are at this point have been able to achieve some of these things, then it does mean that the same can happen to you.

So, onto those benefits.

- You will have a better understanding of your own thoughts and desires.

- You will have new resources to help you to tackle problems in life.
- You will remove or change those bad and distorted thoughts or beliefs.
- You will have improved thought patterns and beliefs.
- You will feel a greater sense of wholeness.
- You will be in tune with the entire mind/body connection.
- You will feel far more grounded.
- You will overcome trauma from your past.
- You will notice a drop in your daily stress levels.
- You will drop those old protective mechanisms that just do not work any longer.
- You will feel stronger in a spiritual sense.
- You will be aware of what actually is your true value.
- You will be able to cope better with life.
- You will notice an improvement in your relationships.
- You will no longer feel such a need to defend yourself constantly.
- You will be more proactive.
- You will drop the need to be reactive.
- You will become mindful and more at peace.
- You will develop a purpose in life rather than just drifting.
- You will become more spontaneous.
- You will develop a greater sense of intuition.
- You will improve your sense of self-awareness.
- You will become aware of your inner strengths.
- You will take power away from your unconscious mind.
- You will feel free.

That is quite a healthy list and clearly people will always get their own benefits from the method since we are indeed all unique. Also, spend some time looking through the list above and see which ones you feel actually apply to you and which you would like to improve on within your own life.

Problems and Conditions that Can be Helped with the Hakomi Method.

At the same time, it has been argued by a number of people that this method has been able to help them with a range of problems and conditions to the point where they feel that they no longer suffer from them. Once again, there is no guarantee that this is going to happen to you, and it also depends on how much effort you put into the method, but checking them out will certainly do you no harm.

- Help with trauma that has so far been untreated.
- Potential for help with PTSD related issues.
- Dealing with depression.
- Dealing with anxiety.
- Dealing with addiction and substance abuse.
- Dealing with attachment issues.
- Increasing energy.
- Helping to resolve issues within relationships.
- Helping you to experience pleasure.
- Improve your view of your own body and own self.
- Helping to overcome severe stress.
- Making it easier to feel calm.
- Making it easier to cope with issues that would normally make you stressed.

As with the benefits, the list is not the finished article, and you will always get out of this method whatever you put into it. Also, it is best to not place too much of an emphasis on this being the sole cure as it can often be the case that this approach merely makes it easier for the doors to open allowing you to explore other avenues that could ultimately lead to you making the progress and improvements that you had always wanted.

As you can imagine, there is quite a lot to get through, so it's best that I see about moving things along a bit.

Chapter 4

The Branches of Hakomi

There are a number of clear branches of Hakomi, and I feel that I need to expand on this to further clarify the points made in the previous chapter. The combination of both Western and Eastern approaches and philosophies is rather interesting. Not only that, but both of those spheres of influence are then sub-divided into further branches to ultimately complete an all-encompassing type of therapy.

Now, as I work through the different branches and spheres of influence within this method, I want you to start working on the reaction that you have when you hear about the various approaches or philosophies. It may be an automatic response for you to immediately state that something does not appeal, but what is it that is causing you to think along those lines? Is it due to a previous experience? Perhaps it is because you have just read or heard things about it and have made your decision that you do not want to know anything else about it?

Well, no matter the reason, I want you to put any pre-conceived ideas to one side as that is key if you are wanting to make any headway with the Hakomi Method.

Humanistic Therapy Approaches.

A substantial part of the entire methodology is connected to what is generally known as humanistic therapy. The aim of this approach is to actively encourage the individual to work on developing a better understanding of their own self alongside accepting and being aware of their own individual feelings. This will then, hopefully, allow the individual to form their own personal meaning of life to them rather than it being shaped by what is around them.

Gestalt Therapy.

Another key area is the use of Gestalt Therapy which is a psychotherapeutic approach that has become more popular in recent decades. It comes from the Gestalt school of thought where the individual is viewed as being a whole, which means a combination of body, mind, and soul. Not only that, but there is the belief that the best way of understanding an individual, or for the individual to understand their own self, is to view it as they are at that moment in time and their current situation.

In addition, it actively encourages a greater sense of self-awareness which can often only being achieved by being in the present. Only by becoming more self-aware of your own self can you then hope to develop and grow as a person with you ultimately reaching your full potential.

However, one key part of Gestalt Therapy that then forms an integral part of the entire Hakomi Method is the belief that our development, and our ability to reach our potential, will often be blocked by our own self. Unfortunately, it seems that we are rather good at allowing negative thoughts and the incorrect pre-conceived ideas to influence our decisions and actions even if they are ultimately the wrong thoughts or actions to then do.

By making these wrong decisions, or even understanding that our thoughts were wrong, it does mean that we have a tendency to feel rather unhappy in our life with this negativity then strengthening those incorrect thoughts to such an extent that it is as if they become the norm.

Gestalt Therapy, and its influence in the Hakomi Method, is to reverse those wrong thoughts and ideas by getting us to turn the spotlight into better areas. You need to be able to view and understand your thoughts and beliefs without being critical of yourself. You must live in the present and understand the here and now concept to ultimately lead to you being capable of being aware of the way that you genuinely think and feel rather than feeling what you believe you are supposed to feel.

Aspects of Buddhism.

The Hakomi Method also incorporates aspects of Buddhism into its teachings, but you must remember that most religious scholars view Buddhism as being more of a philosophy and way of life rather than a religion in the strictest sense. Hopefully that single fact will allow you to effectively drop your guard and allow the method to penetrate into your mind and soul.

The main area of Buddhism that is incorporated into the method is the concept of meditation and mindfulness which, even though it has been adopted by many Western forms of therapy, is Buddhist in its origins.

Of course, this aspect is all about clarifying the mind and meditation is known to work wonders in this area. Not only that, but the theory behind using it within Hakomi is that it then makes it easier for you to focus your mind on the more important things rather than you being distracted by all of this external noise. It is also worth pointing out that Buddhist principles have been used in a variety of psychotherapeutic approaches, so this is hardly unique.

Buddhism spends so much time making you look inwards at your own self and, as a result, self-awareness is key since without it you will be unable to reach Nirvana. Now, the Hakomi Method is not about reaching that blissful state, but it is certainly drawing on the peaceful aspects of the practice and the benefits that then come with it.

Remember it is More Than Just Branches.

This point has tended to surface on several occasions throughout this chapter, as well as those that preceded it, but I need to really stress that the Hakomi Method is about more than just being aware of these different principles and the steps that those principles then effectively make you take.

If you allow yourself to purely focus on these principles on an individual basis, then it stands to reason that you will lose the true essence of what is happening within this methodology. Remember, you are going to learn how to look beyond those automatic thoughts and see where it then leads you to, and if you allow yourself to be drawn into worrying as to whether or not you are following the principles, then you have kind of failed to a certain extent.

Of course, nobody can really fail at this method, but it would certainly alter what you are then going to be able to get out of doing it, and we all want to reach the end of implementing this methodology and form of psychotherapy and believe that we do indeed have a far superior understanding of our own self.

Bringing the Chapter to an End.

My reasoning for mentioning the key spheres of influence in regards to the Hakomi Method is to just provide you with a basic background as to where the creators of the method were drawing their inspiration from and the reasons why. When you look at the different areas and think about the five principles that I mentioned in an earlier chapter, then it all makes absolute sense as to why they have decided to lean so heavily on these influential areas.

By offering a clear explanation of the foundations of the method, it will hopefully come across as being not so scary when you are seeking to take advantage of it and employ the methods in your own life. Of course, that does then mean that you need to be aware of how the method works and how to then use it correctly, so that is where we are going to head off to next.

Chapter 5

How it Works

Understanding how this entire approach works is going to ultimately prove to be rather important in helping you to decide as to whether or not you should proceed with the therapy. The truth is that Hakomi works in a number of different ways, and that is simply because of it incorporating different aspects of psychology and philosophies from around the world as has been shown in previous chapters.

It's important for me to point out that even though this is regarded as being a relatively new method and new approach, the actual ideas and concepts that lie at the root have, at times, been around for a substantially longer period of time. However, it is the way in which different aspects are brought together in a synthesis that is the new aspect.

Also, I want to just state that this method does not exactly come with an approach that is set in stone for you to follow which makes sense as its primary objective is on allowing you the opportunity to explore your own self. Their feeling is that being forced into following a strict approach will also then place additional confines on your mind which is hardly going to help you in finding out more about your own self.

So, what do you need to do to really kick-start this method and begin to get to grips with the way in which it could, potentially at least, change your mind? Well, perhaps we should begin by looking deep within your own thought processes since that is at the core of everything to do with the Hakomi Method.

The Ability to Explore the Depths of Your Mind.

This method has the intention of delving into the depths of your mind in order to change those fundamental ideas that are causing chaos in your life. For some, this approach can appear to be rather difficult, but with Hakomi, the feeling of being safe is placed at the absolute heart of the beginning of any therapy session.

It does make so much sense for safety, and feeling safe, to be so important because without that feeling it is difficult to relax enough to allow those thoughts to come to the fore. If we perceive there to be any danger, then it becomes a natural human instinct for our defences to reach up even higher than ever before in order to protect us. If that happens, then our ability to address those issues diminishes.

With this, the Hakomi Method seeks to teach you on how to lower those guards just enough to allow yourself the space to delve deeper into your mind. It seeks to build confidence within your own self as it is from that confidence that you will then be able to look at yourself from an honest perspective which will ultimately produce the results that you are looking for.

Another negative aspect of your defences being up is that it begins to create a lot of external noise. Any noise will then make it much harder to listen to what is really going on inside of you and to get to grips with the part of you that has created this need to be protected at this moment.

The problem with a lack of safety, at least in our mind, is that we then allow those preconceived ideas to take precedence over everything else even when it does not reflect our true self. I will be returning to this point regarding safety later on in another chapter.

So, how does the method allow you to move deep into your mind? The key points are, in my opinion, as follows.

- It creates a sense of safety and security within your own self.
- It teaches you to drop your guard but remain confident in doing so.
- You learn that the depths of your mind does not have to be a scary place.

Of course, it is still not going to be easy for you at the outset as the very idea of opening up your mind in this manner feels as if it could be impossible, but that is not actually going to be the case.

The Art of Mindfulness.

Being mindful is, for some, easier than it sounds. However, it does take some effort on your part to ultimately get to a point where it almost becomes second nature to you. Yes, it does take time for you to be able to perfect the art, but it has been shown to be beneficial in a number of areas and not just within the realms of the aims of the Hakomi Method.

Within the realms of psychotherapy, being mindful incorporates a number of key approaches that will ultimately lead to you being successful in your approach. This art is never intended to be stressful in any way. Actually, the complete opposite is true as you are turning your attention inwards but in a slow and gentle manner. The only thing is that it needs to be a sustained approach for it to prove to be effective, but this should not be as troubling as you may initially fear.

Not only that, but it also lends itself to an increase in the sensitivity of your senses as well as what is around you incorporated with the manner in which it affects what you are doing. This is seen by some as being a method of simply becoming aware of what is around you since we are generally distracted by the noise going on inside of our mind.

This elimination of external noise that is capable of masking what we really think and feel is central to the method itself being able to work. That is why this part of the process is one of the first things that you need to be capable of doing, or else your mind is just far too busy and complex for you to actually understand what it is that you really feel or desire. If this is impossible for you, then you need to spend time getting to grips with what the method is teaching you to then be able to break through this particular barrier.

Being Aware of Your Body.

Earlier, I mentioned that one of the principles in the Hakomi Method was the way in which the mind and body had to act as one. Of course, to achieve this there is a need for you to even just be aware of what it is that your body is feeling or experiencing at any given time. For some, this does occur when they are becoming more involved in mindfulness as the reduction in that noise will then permit you to turn your focus on other areas, and how your body is feeling can often be one of those areas.

But what do I mean when I say that you need to be aware of your body?

In this approach, it is believed that your body holds an extensive amount of information that has been stored there throughout your life. That means every trauma, emotional and physical pain, happy memories and sad memories are effectively stored in the cells of your body. Ignoring those memories or feelings, especially when the negative issues are more abundant and powerful, will then result in you encountering a number of difficulties and even illness.

This concept is not unique to the Hakomi Method. A number of philosophies, and psychotherapies, also believe that negative emotions can manifest in a physical sense, so that in itself is not unusual. For those that are involved in this approach, there is a feeling that all of this trauma and negativity can become trapped in the body. It will ultimately lead to fatigue, tension in the muscles, chronic pain, anxiety, depression, the list just goes on and on.

So, the Hakomi Method seeks to release that trapped trauma and, in the process of doing so, freeing up not only your body but also your mind. Hopefully, it will then relieve you of a number of the physical and emotional symptoms that have been created by those traumas bringing you a sense of freedom which then, in turn, makes it easier to explore other aspects of your mind and belief systems.

Of course, these are areas that the method focuses on, but I still need to address the way that the entire approach works to make it easier for you to better understand what may very well happen to you.

The Core Assumptions.

There are several core assumptions assimilated with this method, and they all lie at the heart of what you then need to do to ultimately make the kind of progress you were looking for. In fact, these assumptions then lead to the development of the actual therapy and the way that it will be beneficial to you so being aware of them will make it easier to understand the method in general.

First, there is the belief that we store away memories and experiences from the moment that we are born until we get into adulthood. This forms a set of core beliefs that sit deep in our unconscious mind and they effectively make us into who we are, and what we think we believe, as we go through our lives. However, it must be stressed that these are not just things that we make up. Instead, it is directly related to experiences in our life.

As the core assumptions idea evolves, these 'beliefs' begin to influence everything that we both think and do about life in general. Furthermore, it will also affect the way we behave and can have a strong negative impact on how we develop as adults. These thoughts and core beliefs are so powerful that they can simply crush what we truly feel, if only we were allowing ourselves to listen to those thoughts.

The problem with these beliefs, and this is part of psychotherapy in general and not just the Hakomi Method is that the beliefs get to a point where they no longer serve us. It is accepted that they may very well have protected us at some point in the past, but they will eventually turn against us and hamper our ability to live the kind of life that we wanted.

These core assumptions, and actively tackling them, is perhaps the most important aspect of the entire method and that is why so much time is spent on resolving these incorrect beliefs or thoughts. The ability to make any kind of noticeable progress is firmly entrenched with the need to tackle these thoughts and beliefs as quickly as possible. The only problem that you may then encounter is simply the way in which you may require some additional help from a third-party to assist you in really starting things off on the correct foot.

Bringing the Chapter to an End.

The main reason for this chapter has been to effectively prepare you for moving into the method itself. You now understand the concept of core assumptions and the way in which they play a key role in the way that we think and act at this point.

For me, the best way to really get into this method is by focusing on the areas that I have discussed throughout this chapter. Your body, your mind, and those assumptions all come together and dictate the way that you live your life, which may not even be the way that you want to live. I hope that you at least feel a certain sense of excitement at what may follow, but at the same time I understand the apprehension that must also surround you because you are venturing into somewhere new, and that can be scary for a number of people.

However, as you are about to see, getting started and putting certain things into action is going to be less stressful than you had perhaps imagined.

Chapter 6

Getting Started

My hope is that, by now, you are at the stage where you just want to get started with your own therapy, but I do have to stress one key point. Prior to starting, it is essential that you are aware of what your own aims are going to be with your therapy. You see, there's a need to understand the changes that you hope therapy brings to you, and perhaps even have a basic understanding of why you feel the way that you do about various things.

As with any method that incorporates any of the principles that I have mentioned above, the key to getting started is in your preparation. You need to be ready, and willing, to accept changes that will ultimately be beneficial to you even if they are uncomfortable at the start. Now, the different things that I am going to discuss do not have to be done in any particular order, but each thing is central to the Hakomi Method and it is important, for the sake of this form of psychotherapy, for you to work through each point to ultimately provide yourself with the best opportunity of making progress.

So, here is what I want you to do.

Finding the Correct Therapist.

Even though there are many aspects of this method that you can do all on your own, it can often be beneficial to at least kick things off by meeting with a trained therapist in this method. However, we are all different in what we are looking for with a therapist, so there is no single solution that will be guaranteed to help everybody.

It is essential that you feel that there is a bond between you both as that will inspire confidence in you from the outset. Furthermore, confidence makes it easier for you to carry out the rather difficult task of turning your view inwards and really get to those inner thoughts and feelings that are causing you all of the problems. Remember, having the confidence to do that, and feeling safe while you make these attempts, is at the heart of the Hakomi Method and getting to the bottom of those core assumptions.

The correct therapist for you will be an individual that makes you feel safe and also someone that you feel you can respect. The confidence that you get from those two feelings will then make it substantially easier to communicate with your unconscious mind and to directly contend with your issues.

What Makes You Feel Safe?

In the previous chapter, I mentioned the need for you to feel safe as being a basic premise of this entire approach, so in order to get started with the method you need to be aware of what makes you feel safe. This concept also applies if you are planning on visiting an Hakomi therapist as they should go out of their way to create this feeling from the beginning.

What is it that you seek in order to feel safe with an individual? It can be many different things for people from their mannerisms, the sound of their voice, body language, how they cope when faced with your understandable anxieties or incorrect thoughts, the list just goes on forever.

So, before you go any further, I want you to just take a moment to block out that external noise and really focus on what it is that you need to feel safe. Only by understanding this will you then be able to locate the correct therapist for your needs allowing for greater improvement over a shorter period of time.

Becoming Deaf to Noise.

You will have noticed a recurring theme whereby I discuss this external noise, but it is so powerful and detrimental to your ability to do anything that I need to mention it over and over again.

The external noise that we are all subjected to can deafen us to such an extent that it forces us into making wrong decisions. When you then incorporate those incorrect and damaging internal thoughts with the noise, you then have something that is very powerful and is clearly going to work against your ability to make progress in your life.

But first, before you seek to become deaf to the noise, you need to first of all notice it for what it truly is to you. The noise itself is going to be unique to every single one of us, so some work is involved. Ultimately, it goes back to the idea of mindfulness and being in the moment, so at first you need to stop what you are doing and look at just slowing down every single aspect to allow you to take stock of what is really going on.

The problem is that we fail to notice the noise to begin with. To us, it has become the norm and that is the process we need to reverse. This is something that can only be achieved by working at it on our own. We need to make a concerted effort to just stop and pay attention to our own selves right down to the small and apparently insignificant things we often ignore. This can be the smallest of intrusive thoughts or even slight movements that we have now come to take for granted. It is only by focusing on those things that we can indeed start to become deaf to the noise that surrounds us.

Being Aware of What You Need to Change.

No form of psychotherapy is going to be able to be successful if the individual themselves are blissfully unaware of what it is that they want to change. It does not matter how big or small the issue may be, or even how many things that you would like to be different as the key is in knowing what you would like your end goals to be.

What is it about your life that you are not content with? What kind of thoughts do you have that you would love to put to bed once and for all? What actions do you wish you could alter and yet you somehow fail to have the mental fortitude to do so?

Remember, this does not have to involve you making wholesale changes to your entire life; it can be much smaller than that. However, you should be aware of the problems and the way you would prefer things to be if you are to ever make progress.

What are Your Strongest Emotions?

The Hakomi Method is all about being in the moment and reaching an understanding of your emotions and feelings. So, with that in mind it can be useful to be aware of those emotions that are actually the strongest that you face. Often, those strong emotions can affect you negatively, so in accordance with psychotherapy they do need to be actioned upon to then remove their power.

Of course, the issue is often that people are not in tune with their emotions, at least not beyond a superficial level, or they are only in tune when they are faced with a crisis. Well, this is about averting those crisis moments by tackling the incorrect beliefs and assumptions that we all have and that are all holding us back.

Becoming More Self-Aware.

Without the concept of self-awareness, you have nothing in this form of therapy, but the same can be said for virtually any form of psychotherapy. However, you will be able to start doing this when you begin working on that external noise and simply noticing your emotions at any given moment.

Hakomi accepts that this is going to take some time and that it will often be uncomfortable, but that will be overcome as you build your sense of safety and security. In doing so, you can delve deeper into your own self and you will indeed become more self-aware than ever before. By the time you repeat the actions of this method on several occasions, you will then discover that being self-aware is fulfilling and will ultimately lead you onto a better path and, as a result, a better life more along the lines that you want it to be.

Taking the First Step.

So, you have spent some time trying to turn the camera inwards rather than outwards. There is a pretty good chance that you are not too happy with what you see, so it is indeed time for you to take that first step.

Of course, you have already done this simply by coming to terms with the simple fact that you need to make some kind of change in your life. The Hakomi Method is, therefore, a lot easier than you were perhaps expecting, but clearly there is still some work to be done if the therapy itself is going to prove to be beneficial to you.

Bringing the Chapter to an End.

The key to getting started with the Hakomi Method is to understand that you can no longer continue to dwell in the past. You must look at how you are feeling at this moment in time and seek to understand what it is that makes you feel safe. The only way in which you will be capable of making progress is by creating that feeling. Only then will you develop the confidence, and ability to become even more self-aware to then lead to significant change.

However, breaking things down into smaller steps and a further explanation of various concepts is going to prove to be useful.

Chapter 7

Breaking it Down Into Small Steps

In the previous chapters, I have sought to get you ready for introducing the basic concepts of this method into your life. However, it can often be daunting to get started as you may wonder where you can even begin, and this is stressful and clearly goes against everything that you are aiming for with this method.

So, I need to counteract that.

What I'm going to do in this chapter is provide you with some small steps and simple exercises that I want you to use on a daily basis. By doing so, it will get you to a point where you feel ready to really adopt the key strategies into your life and start to make significant strides forward. Don't worry, this will not be as difficult as it may initially sound. However, let's begin this chapter by looking more at what you should expect from your initial session with a therapist that is versed in this approach.

Your First Session with a Therapist.

The first thing you will notice is that a Hakomi therapy session does tend to start out in the same way as any other therapy session. That alone should hopefully make you feel less stressed and confident that you can go on to achieve some pretty cool things.

This first session is an opportunity for both yourself and the therapist to basically get to know one another. Your history will be taken, or even just help to allow you to better understand your own history, and to identify the areas that you wish to change or improve in your life. After all, knowing what you want your end result to be will make it easier for everybody to then start off on the correct path.

But what if you have more than one thing that is troubling you? Well, if this is the case then you should look at trying to place the issues in order of importance. The most pressing issue should always be dealt with first as it can often be the case that other issues will then rectify themselves as a result of you being able to change your assumptions and core beliefs in this main area.

After the First Session.

After the first session, you should be more aware of the direction in which you will be heading, but I also need to help you along your way if you plan on incorporating the Hakomi Method into your life all on your own. Remember, this may very well be the approach that works best for you, and it may very well be the case that you will achieve the same fantastic results as you would have done going the therapy route.

However, in both cases you should rather quickly get to a point where you know what you need to do in order to make progress. You should feel content with the issues that you wish to address, and you are aware of those that are causing you the most problems.

If you are doing the therapy approach, then after the first session there should always be some time spent discovering how you are doing, feeling, and what you are thinking before the second session starts. Even if you are tackling things on your own, this concept of going back over any potential progress or identifying new hurdles will help you to break down the barriers rather than allowing them to grow even taller in your mind. There is also a sense that this provides you with some focus, but just doing so will not allow you to make the progress that you require.

Relaxation.

Any session, even on your own, requires absolute relaxation on your part so learning how to make yourself relaxed is going to play a key role at the outset. You may wish to consider these steps just to help you along.

1. Focus on your breathing will instantly help to settle down both your mind and body. There is a reason why breathing exercises are so important in yoga and meditation, and it is purely because of the way in which it does help you to relax as well as taking your mind off other issues that could be creating anxiety and stress.

2. Relaxing your body even just by visualising the muscles in each part becoming less tense will also help you in focusing your mind on matters that are healthier and more wholesome for you rather than the external noise that surrounds you.

3. Using guided imagery has also been shown to be a useful tool in allowing you to get your mind in-tune with the therapy session that is about to begin. This is where it borrows quite heavily from hypnosis and even if you plan on using the method on your own it is still possible for you to create a certain pathway in your mind that helps when it comes to the guidance aspect.

Dealing with Mind and Body Awareness.

Mind and body awareness is key, so no matter if you are in a therapy session or looking at performing various aspects of this method on your own, you need to be aware of how to ultimately notice both your body and mind.

There are several ways in which this can be done via the Hakomi Method. Often, it will involve you closing your eyes and attempting to become aware of what it is that you are feeling in the present moment both physically as well as mentally. This is where this method differs from a number of other forms of psychotherapy in that it very much deals with how you are feeling, or thinking, at this exact moment in time. Other therapies will focus primarily on the past, and even though that is still important, it is the awareness of the here and now that is key.

So, what does your therapist hope will happen when you begin to focus on how you are at this moment? Well, the method puts forward several potential scenarios that could occur, but you should try to maintain a sense of being curious as to what it all means as that will then allow you to explore things further.

It is hoped that as you become aware of your feelings and emotions that perhaps a certain emotion, or memory, or image will come to the fore. It may even be as subtle as a movement in your posture as even this can often indicate that there are issues beneath the surface that need to be addressed.

Should you notice anything such as this happening, then the method teaches you to explore that emotion, thought, or whatever it may be and to be curious about it. This is about more than just acknowledging that it is there as it is more to do with delving deeper into it but in such a way that you are not just giving lip service to it or allowing it to completely take over your mind.

But Why Pay Attention?

As most psychotherapies focus on the past, it does then come across as being slightly different in paying so much attention to something that you are feeling at this moment in time. However, that is because there is the belief that by paying attention to whatever it is that you are experiencing, that you will then be able to actually access your unconscious mind. Obviously, that is where the problems can be found, and the Hakomi Method is all about removing as much of the power from your unconscious mind as possible.

As you learn how to access your unconscious mind, it means that you will then be capable of developing a better understanding of those core beliefs that are located deep within your unconscious mind. Once you are able to do that, you can challenge those beliefs that are working against you and start to remove the influence that they hold.

Accept Instead of Judge.

Since Hakomi is primarily based on mindfulness, there is then the idea that you are more focused on acceptance rather than going out to judge your thoughts and emotions. Being self-critical in this way is completely contradictory to what the method is about.

So, what does this mean when you have that thought or feeling or even an image before you? It means you should be looking at it not in a critical sense, but with love and compassion. Do not view it as a negative thing that has happened to you, but instead seek to tell yourself that you are loved and that the thought itself once served a purpose. You should ultimately give it thanks for what it did for you, but remind it that it is no longer required in the same manner.

The intention is for you to be able to correctly process these thoughts and ideas so that they are no longer the same hindrance as they are at this point. Of course, by focusing on them during these quiet, and relaxing, moments is important since it eliminates that external noise, which is always key within this method.

The hope is that this proves to be the best way for you to make those positive transformations that we are all seeking, and if it involves tackling a number of different issues independently of one another, then that should no longer be regarded as being a problem.

The Commitment.

Any practitioner or individual that is looking to use this method has to be willing to go ahead and use the methods and techniques for an extended period of time to get the results that they are seeking. There is a need for commitment for their own self and this has to be consistent to get anywhere. Of course, all you are doing is having that commitment towards your own personal growth and the understanding that we are all a work in progress, but that it does get easier the more you look inwards and deal with the difficulties that used to plague us.

Clearly, any form of psychotherapy requires this commitment so it is hardly new, but this is something that will be in the forefront of your mind throughout this process. However, it is not meant to be a stressful situation but rather a source of pride and comfort that you are tackling those negative core assumptions and creating brand new ones that are more beneficial to you at this moment in your life.

An Open View to Change.

As well as being committed, there is also a need for you to have an open view towards changing your own self. There needs to be that acceptance that all is not well, for whatever reason that may be, and that there is a need for things to be different. There must also be an acceptance that the only way in which things can change is by looking within your own self. It has to come from you, but you cannot be critical and judge yourself in a negative manner as that is going to be counter-productive.

Being open to change should be exciting and you should feel something akin to a rush of adrenaline when you just think about it. The freedom that comes from releasing your mind and body from these negative thoughts and experiences is exhilarating and one that should be embraced. If you are closed to this idea, or you feel that anxiety is taking over, then to be honest dealing with that feeling of anxiety should be your first port of call and the first thing to ultimately tackle via this method.

Integrating Into Daily Life.

The final step that I would like to mention at this point is the need for integrating your new experiences and way of thinking into daily life. Up until this moment in time, you have been working hard at running your life via what is ultimately an incorrect way of thinking. This leads to poor decisions being taken that continue to just strengthen the incorrect way of thinking so you do eventually get nowhere.

Whether it is via a therapist or on your own, there is very much a need for you to be aware of how to integrate the Hakomi Method and what it teaches you into daily life. It is only by doing this that you can then hope to make the progress you were looking for, and once you get that ball rolling then the rest will become substantially easier.

So, what do you do?

Well, the answer is very personal to you as it is all related to the issues that are of concern and the way in which you have replaced those poor thoughts with something far more positive. However, the starting block is often looking at your new thoughts compared to your old and the areas of your life where you were being restricted as a result. By thinking about what your new approach ultimately means regards not feeling the same way about situations will allow you to begin to see new possibilities.

Of course, there is then the need for you to go after those new possibilities as merely thinking about them and believing that it would be nice is not enough. You have already looked at taking action by tackling your incorrect thoughts, but that action has to go an additional step for it to really be as effective as it could be.

In other words, this is not about trying to incorporate it into daily life by offering you a series of tasks. Instead, it relies on you coming to terms with the areas of your life where you were once inhibited and understanding that this is not the case.

What I would recommend, if you find yourself in this exact situation, is to even consider making a list of areas where there used to be some difficulties. Place yourself in that actual moment and determine what it was that was so difficult, the feelings, the emotions, memories whatever it may be. Identify them to then rectify them, or even just to remind yourself that you have already carried out the work in that area and that the issue have vanished forever.

Look at your daily routine and think about every step of the day. Allow yourself to mentally travel there and guide yourself through the day. Think about how, upon reaching a certain point, you would always choose one particular road, a road that may have protected you and yet did not deliver to you what you had hoped. Now, look at your new road that has been created thanks to the work that you have done in coming to terms with negative feelings and thoughts. Envision the positive vibes and ideas that surround this road compared to the old way of thinking. Hopefully, your new road is full of positivity and sunshine whereas the old is broken and dark.

Practice Makes Perfect.

The only problem that some individuals have with any form of psychotherapy is that it is very repetitive. Just saying that you understand something once is not enough. You need to put action into it and do so over and over again until it becomes second nature.

This is something that is not unique to the Hakomi Method, but it links in with the concept of dynamic mindfulness where you reach a point that you are constantly aware of what you are feeling and the reasons why. Remember that you are often tackling core assumptions that have been with you since you were a child, so it is not going to simply go away in a short period of time, unless you are exceptionally lucky, so there has to be a willingness to practice and practice as much as required.

Once again, you should never judge your own self or be critical if you notice that you have slipped back into your old way of thinking as that will serve no purpose whatsoever. Instead, accept that it has happened and seek to understand why by listening to your feelings and emotions at that point. By seeking out the answer, you can then potentially avoid making that mistake again.

Bringing the Chapter to an End.

The main reason for this chapter was to show you the way in which the method develops from those initial feelings of safety and security to building a feeling of trust with either a therapist or your own self, to coming to terms with your thoughts and emotions. They are all logical steps, and they are ones that need to be undertaken to allow you to make the progress that you need to make.

However, there is no sense of failure within the Hakomi Method as everything is personal to you and others can only offer you guidance. The only thing is that you are honest and open with yourself to then allow you to make the progress that you need to make. Without that, you have nothing.

So, the steps are there merely to guide you rather than as a set of instructions. Whether or not you use them is entirely up to you as the key is in you reaching your desired goal no matter the path that you eventually take to get there.

Chapter 8

The Flow

In this chapter, I'm going to focus on something that is often referred to as being the flow of the method. While each session is unique in its own right, there is a tendency for there to be a general flow that is followed with the method. Of course, if you are looking at using this method on your own then not every aspect is going to apply. However, you can still take individual snippets from the flow and adapt them into your very own strategy. Also, never see this as being set in stone as there is no aspect of this therapy that takes that approach.

I will quickly look at each step and offer an explanation as to what is meant by it.

1. Establishing a therapeutic relationship that has its roots in both respect and warmth.

This first point will follow quite naturally into point two, and it is easy to understand why there is a need for a therapist and client to have this feeling of respect and warmth towards one another. Failure to do so will only lead to that external noise being turned up a few notches on the dial making the entire process far more difficult than it needs to be.

A feeling of mutual respect for one another as human beings, as well as never being critical of one another and their choices, manages to lower those barriers and it opens up the door for progress to be made.

2. Develop the concept of safety in the relationship by being attuned to one another.

I have mentioned safety on a regular basis and you can see how it does run nicely with the first point. Not only is there a need to be attuned to one another, but the therapist and client also need to make it evident to the other individual that they are present in the moment. Any lapse in focus can, and often will, be read in a negative manner and make it harder for that progress to be made.

Furthermore, this can also be applied to your own self simply because you must feel safe within your own mind as well as being in tune with those inner thoughts to then be able to start to overcome them and help them to lose some of their power.

3. Develop the concept of mindful awareness.

Once the individual feels safe and that feeling of warmth and respect has been established, either the therapist or individual themselves will need to begin to develop their own concept of mindful awareness. Clearly, this is designed to bring them into the present moment and to begin to eliminate the external noise that is causing all of these problems. Becoming aware of your surroundings and your own thoughts will always form the basis of this part of the method.

Mindfulness is, to many, a form of meditation and it has its roots in Buddhist practices that stretch back into history. It slows the mind and allows the individual to not detach from their surroundings but to grow accustomed to seeing what is before them and the impact it has on their spirit and soul.

4. Conduct little experiments.

This part of the method is something that can be done either on your own or via a therapist. There is often the fear of people stagnating when it comes to their therapy, and while it can be due to a number of reasons there is a sense that it can often come by not pushing yourself enough. Now, this method does not tell you to go out there and put yourself in stressful situations to basically smash through your issues due to being in an extremely uncomfortable situation. Instead, these experiments are more about gauging how you are progressing with your incorrect core beliefs.

So, what are some of the experiments that you can do?

There are a number of things that can be tried. First, you need to continually check to see how easily you can get into tune with the way that you are feeling, or what you are experiencing, in the present moment. Just allow another thought to creep into your mind that effectively tells you how easy or difficult it was for you to become mindful.

Also, if you are attending therapy, then the therapist could conduct an experiment whereby they effectively carry out the method or technique on their own self in front of you. This kind of example can, at times, make it easier to then apply the same methods to your own situation with it reducing the stress levels that are often attached to different aspects of therapy.

Experiments to Provoke Experiences.

One of the keys is to discover ways in which experiences and the emotions or feelings attached to them can be felt in the present moment. By doing this, it allows the individual, or therapist, to make a better decision as to how to then go ahead and tackle them and finally put those negative aspects to bed once and for all.

This can be done via experiments, and even though they are not guaranteed to work or to get the reaction that you are seeking, they are still very important within this method.

The experiments are to largely recreate moments and to allow some habitual tension to arise to then allow the individual to identify it. This is often done at the beginning of an individual delving into the method as it does then become easier to dip into the unconscious mind whenever you want to tackle a feeling and to ultimately resolve it.

Another experiment is referred to 'movement patterns' which links into the knowledge that when we are uncomfortable that we have a tendency to make certain movements that show our inner feelings. By recreating them, we stand a chance of then creating the experiences and emotions that come with those movements allowing us to then identify them and tackle them head-on.

5. Learning Dynamic Mindfulness.

The Hakomi Method is not just about being mindful from the point of view of meditation, instead they have effectively pioneered the concept of dynamic mindfulness. Some may prefer to call it active mindfulness. In addition, it is seen as being a method by which you can get to the preferred state of mind quickly, but safely.

The intention is to effectively be mindful on a constant basis, as opposed to the more meditative state of mind where it occurs whenever you want even though it is then in a controlled environment. You need to learn to live it since by doing so you eliminate so much of the external noise and also reduce the power of our core beliefs as they are constantly being challenged and being shown for what they are really worth, which is nothing.

6. Transformation.

Transformation is clearly important because without the ability to transform and change things, then the lower the chances of you being able to get anywhere in your life. Within Hakomi, this is done by not being angry towards those core concepts, but to accept that they exist and then look at removing as much of their power as possible while perhaps even replacing them with something that is a lot healthier.

The actual transformation process has a tendency to run along familiar lines.

First, you identify that emotion or physical feeling.

Next, you examine the core material that lies behind it.

Next, you process what you are thinking and feeling to further develop your understanding.

You seek to integrate new experiences to replace that negative core.

The greater the number of new experiences replacing the old, then the greater the transformation.

OK, it sounds easier than it is, but the entire method just gets you to identify those feelings and to challenge them in a non-confrontational manner to see if they are still actually true for you today. If not, then the method entices you to change those feelings and thoughts for something that is helpful and reflects who you are at this moment in time. It is effectively wiping the slate clean one bad thought or feeling at a time and replacing it with a more positive and uplifting event that you will actually enjoy referring back to over and over again.

7. The Ability to Move Forward.

Finally, there has to be a sense whereby you feel that you are able to move forward after challenging each thought. The failure to do so will just mean that you are stuck in the past, which is something that the Hakomi Method does not really deal with.

However, within this realm of psychotherapy, the intention is that those positive thoughts and transformations will become so strong that they simply over-power the old material without you doing much. So, when you catch yourself developing a certain negative thought or physical sensation, then you will get to the point where you can identify it, understand that you have already been fortunate enough to deal with it, and that the issues in your mind and within every cell in your body has been rectified.

In other words, you will be able to breathe and just not give the power to those negative aspects. By repeating that process over and over again, their power will vanish and your new way of thinking will then become the norm.

Bringing the Chapter to an End.

There are a number of other components of this method that I have not included in this method, but then this entire book is designed to just get you interested in the method and to then be willing to explore things further. The flow, in that respect, has been simplified somewhat to give you the basic steps that everybody will have to work through to get to their desired end result. There is no time limit or time constraints, so that will immediately remove some of the pressure and stress that you are under with it, therefore, making it easier for you to make progress.

Chapter 9

Understanding the Method

I accept that the earlier chapters are covering different parts of the method, so I felt that the final chapter should really be more of a summary and looking back at the most important aspects of the method. By doing so, I hope that you will then have a clearer understanding of what is involved with you then potentially being excited at the thought of applying it in your own life.

The Method Changes Core Material.

I have mentioned this idea of core assumptions and beliefs on a number of occasions, but it is truly central to the Hakomi Method. The approach believes that this core material can consist of a number of different forms of media including images, sounds, emotional dispositions, distinct memories, neural patterns, and so many other things.

From this, practitioners of this method believe that these core memories and materials are then able to influence us in their own unique way. In short, they will effectively shape our own general belief systems, our way of seeing the world, the way we behave, our habits in life, and even the way in which we react to various situations. In other words, they are powerful, which is why they need to be tackled and changed when they are working against us in our life.

The difficulty with these assumptions is that they are able to really exert their influence often in an unconscious manner. The problem is that we may not even initially be aware of what is going on until it is too late and those beliefs or way of behaving are effectively set into stone. However, it is generally accepted that they can go on to influence our life in a number of ways.

They will be capable of altering our response to feeling safe, our sense of belonging somewhere, the way we approach responsibility, how we deal with power, love, our sexuality, our appreciation for others, it can alter absolutely fundamental aspects of our character that then go on to shape the way that we live our life. You can see how incorrect ways of thinking could then have a detrimental impact on our future.

Hakomi and the Core Material.

What the method teaches us is that there are two schools of thought when it comes to these beliefs. There is the understanding that some do indeed work for us, such as do not cross the road when there is traffic, but others limit us and are actually rather disabling. Hakomi teaches you how to distinguish between the two, so that those that stress you and make you anxious are removed from the equation while those that do indeed protect you are left alone.

The Experiential Psychotherapy.

To some, the idea of experiential psychotherapy sounds scary just from the name alone, but to others it could be quite an exciting time and something that you can really get your teeth into.

However, all it means is that this form of psychotherapy deals with the present only and does not then dwell on the past, unlike other therapies out there. You learn how to use your feelings and emotions as they are at this moment in time to then gain access to the core material that is often powering the way you think and act.

By accessing these thoughts, and understanding how they make you feel at this exact moment in time allows you to then make the appropriate changes in the immediate. By doing so, you will then be able to notice the changes and the way in which they do indeed improve your life. Once you are able to achieve this on just a single occasion, and then realize the boost to your life, it will then become easier to make additional changes later on.

A Body-Somatic Psychotherapy.

Furthermore, it is referred to as being a body-somatic psychotherapy and this may also require some additional explanation to help you understand how this could very well help you.

Within the Hakomi Method, along with other forms of psychotherapy, there is the belief that your body is a special resource that is able to both reflect and store those core beliefs and memories that form them. By accessing them, it allows you to get to that core material and hope to make changes since it is reflected in the way in which your body reacts, or feels, at any given time.

The difficulty, according to the practitioners of this method, is that people do not pay enough attention to the actual reasons as to why their body is feeling a certain way. Those aches and pains, or general fatigue, is often cast aside with comments that we have been doing too much, or we are just getting old.

The Hakomi Method believes that this is not always the case. Instead, it goes deeper than all of that as, for them, the mind and body connection is so powerful that one does indeed directly influence the other. By teaching you how to listen to what it is that your body is saying, it then makes sense that you will be able to come to terms with the root of it all and make the changes that are required.

The Present and Felt Experience.

This is another part of the method that I have stressed at various times because the present and felt experience is the only way in which you are then going to be able to make the changes that are required within your own self. You need to become aware of how you are feeling or what you are experiencing at that point, which is certainly not easy at first.

These present experiences or feelings can appear spontaneously or you may be required to, metaphorically at least, poke them with a stick until they emerge and you are able to then identify them. This is achieved via some of the experiments that were mentioned in the previous chapter.

Bringing the Chapter to an End.

If we are to effectively bring this chapter to an end, then what better way than to go ahead and just say that the entire Hakomi Method has three main aims that you will hopefully achieve throughout this process.

First, you will work towards a point in your life, either on your own or via a therapist, whereby you can become more self-aware of your existence and the emotions and feelings that you have surrounding you.

Next, you will then use the methodologies that we have explored throughout the chapters that form the Hakomi Method in order to work on developing those experiences in the present moment to then correctly address those issues and allow you to work on organizing and refuting those in-built assumptions.

Finally, your focus will be on effectively healing those core aspects and removing those that no longer work for you but rather against you as they no longer serve any purpose.

You have to admit, if you are able to achieve all of this, then your life is going to end up working out for the better.

Conclusion

There is little doubt that the Hakomi Method does have a number of interesting concepts that can be incorporated into your daily life. However, as with any method that focuses on your mind and actions, how much you get out of it depends on the effort that you put in.

Throughout this book, I have tried to show the ways in which you can begin to bring it into your life. I admit that it takes work, and you will trip up along the way, but this is an approach to life that can undoubtedly bring a number of benefits to you.

For many, this is a completely new way of trying to bring some inner peace to your mind and body, and it can have an impact if you simply believe in it. Of course, what you get from it is going to coincide with the amount of effort and belief that you put into adopting and understanding the method, but this is not something where we can either pass or fail.

The Hakomi Method is not a step-by-step guide that will guarantee that you find that inner peace. It comes to the conclusion that we are all our own self, and it is up to us to find that end result no matter what it may be, or even how long it takes.

Remember that this is clearly a voyage that you are going to go on, and it is one that should be embraced due to the positive outcomes that are possible. It will not allow you to become mired in the past or living stuck in those old memories that do not serve any role or work for you. Instead, it helps you in the present moment and to deal with the situations as they arise.

However, it does admit that previous thoughts and beliefs are, in effect, acting as a trigger and that this is going to prove to be detrimental to your overall well-being. By understanding this, and not merely giving them lip service, it means that you will be able to eventually over-ride those incorrect beliefs and go on to think about things in a more positive manner.

Yes, this is going to prove to be hard work, but if you feel that you are stuck and making no progress whatsoever, then just think about how exciting life can be if you are suddenly released and free from those horrible thoughts. You must admit that life would then take on a completely different light if that was to be the case.

Be brave and accept that now is the time to change. Accept that the Hakomi Method may very well be the form of psychotherapy that will ultimately work for you. However, even if you only manage to achieve some small differences in your life, as long as they are for the positive then it does mean that it will have all been worth your while.

One last thing. How would you like winning **a $200.00 Amazon Gift card** and helping us improve this book in the process with a little bit of feedback?

That's right :)

Your opinion is so valuable to us that we are giving away a $200 gift card to the luckiest *one of 200 participants*!

It will only take a minute of your time to let us know what you like and what you didn't like about this book. The hardest part is deciding how to spend the two hundred dollars!

Just follow this link.

http://reviewers.win/somatotherapy

[page intentionally left blank]

www.ingramcontent.com/pod-product-compliance
Lightning Source LLC
Chambersburg PA
CBHW031422250726
48656CB00002B/790

* 9 7 8 1 9 7 7 0 3 6 4 7 6 *